ELITE MILITARY FORCES

THE GREEN BERETS

by Jennifer M. Besel

Consultants:
Major Emanuel Ortiz, Public Affairs Officer, U.S. Army Special Forces Command (Airborne)
Major David Butler, Public Affairs Officer, John F. Kennedy Special Warfare Center and School
Lisa C. Moore, Public Affairs Specialist, U.S. Army SOC Public Affairs Office
Fort Bragg, North Carolina

CAPSTONE PRESS
a capstone imprint

First Facts is published by Capstone Press,
151 Good Counsel Drive, P.O. Box 669, Mankato, Minnesota 56002.
www.capstonepub.com

Books published by Capstone Press are manufactured with paper
containing at least 10 percent post-consumer waste.

Library of Congress Cataloging-in-Publication Data
Besel, Jennifer M.
  The Green Berets / by Jennifer M. Besel.
    p. cm.—(First facts. Elite military forces)
  Includes bibliographical references and index.
  Summary: "Provides information on the U.S. Green Berets, including their training,
missions, and equipment"—Provided by publisher.
  ISBN 978-1-4296-5379-4 (library binding)
  1. United States. Army. Special Forces—Juvenile literature. I. Title. II. Series.
  UA34.S64B47 2011
  356'.16—dc22
                                                    2010029386

Editorial credits:
Christine Peterson, editor; Matt Bruning, designer; Laura Manthe, production specialist

Photo credits:
DOD photo by Sgt. 1st Class Rodney Jackson, U.S. Army, 19; Shutterstock/Jackson
Gee, cover, RCPPHOTO, 17(helmet with NVG); U.S. Air Force photo by Tech. Sgt.
Mike Buytas, 11; U.S. Army photo by SGT Keith D. Henning, 5, Sgt. 1st Class Andrew
Kosterman/1st SFG(A) PAO, 9; U.S. Army Special Operations Command, 6, 13, 14, 21;
U.S. Marine Corps photo by Cpl. Christopher R. Rye, 17(rifle)

Artistic Effects
iStockphoto/Brett Charlton, Craig DeBourbon; Shutterstock/koh sze kiat, Maksym
Bondarchuk, Masonjar, Péter Gudella, reventon2527, Serg64, Tom Grundy

Printed in the United States of America in Melrose Park, Illinois.
092010   005935LKS11

TABLE OF CONTENTS

GREEN BERETS IN ACTION

A team of Green Berets moves through Afghanistan. In the distance, they spot a group of Taliban fighters. A battle breaks out between the two sides. The U.S. soldiers defend their position, but the enemy fights back.

Taliban: an army in Afghanistan that uses terror to spread its ideas

The Green Berets lead an Afghan army toward the enemy. Black smoke fills the air as the **firefight** continues. The Taliban fighters **retreat**.

The Green Berets know this won't be their last battle. They are here to fight enemies of the United States.

firefight: exchange of weapon fire between two military units

retreat: to move away

A POWERFUL TEAM

"Green Beret" is a nickname for soldiers in the U.S. Army's Special Forces. The name comes from their dark green hats. Special Forces soldiers are among the U.S. Army's most highly trained men. Green Berets work with foreign leaders to catch **terrorists**. They train armies in other countries to defend their own lands.

> **terrorist:** someone who uses violence to achieve a goal

Green Berets sneak into enemy territory. They destroy enemy weapons and rescue **hostages**. These soldiers also spy on the enemy's actions. The information they gather helps the Army defend the United States.

hostage: a person held prisoner by an enemy

EARNING THE GREEN BERET

Soldiers who want to wear the green beret must complete tough training. First they need to pass Special Forces Assessment and Selection (SFAS). This 24-day training pushes soldiers to their limits. They have to run, march, and cross **obstacle courses** with almost no sleep.

> **obstacle course:** a series of barriers that a soldier must jump over, climb, or crawl through

FACT

SFAS is so tough the Army offers a class to help soldiers get ready for the training.

FACT

Current U.S. military rules allow only men to serve in Special Forces.

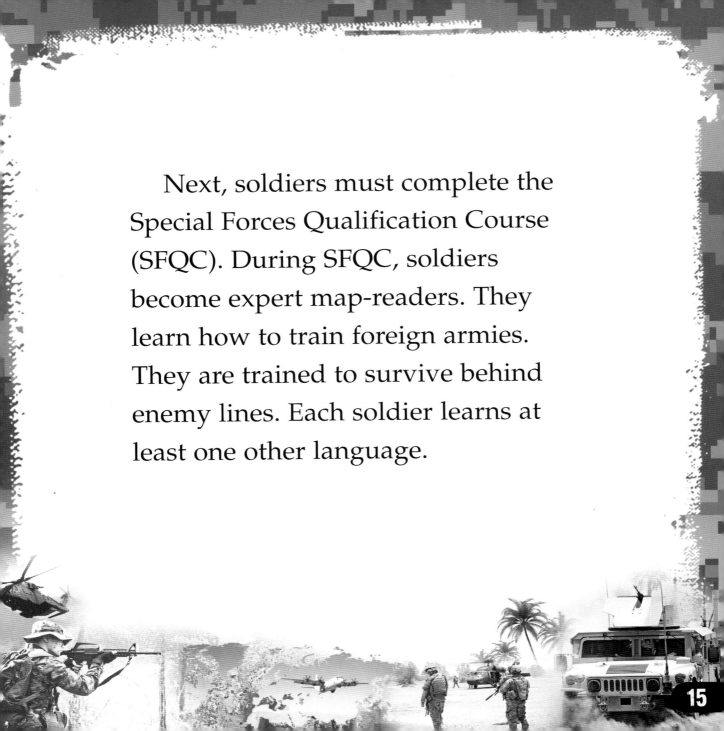

Next, soldiers must complete the Special Forces Qualification Course (SFQC). During SFQC, soldiers become expert map-readers. They learn how to train foreign armies. They are trained to survive behind enemy lines. Each soldier learns at least one other language.

Special Forces teams use high-tech tools. Each soldier carries an M-4 carbine rifle. Night-vision goggles help them see in the dark. Green Berets also carry **Global Positioning Systems** (GPS). They use GPS to mark locations of enemy weapons or hideouts.

Global Positioning System:
a satellite system that determines any location in the world

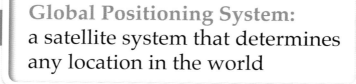

FACT

Green Berets work in teams of 12 men.

night-vision goggles

M-4 carbine rifle

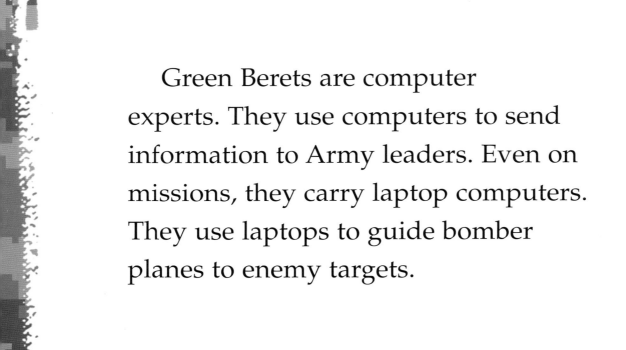

Green Berets are computer experts. They use computers to send information to Army leaders. Even on missions, they carry laptop computers. They use laptops to guide bomber planes to enemy targets.

Special Forces soldiers are experts on weapons used in other countries.

A VERY SPECIAL FORCE

Green Berets are some of the best soldiers in the world. They go deep into enemy lands to protect the United States. They teach armies in other countries how to stop terrorists. Whatever the job, Green Berets are trained and ready to serve.

FACT

At any time, Special Forces teams are on missions in more than 100 countries.

GLOSSARY

firefight (FIRE-fite)—an exchange of weapon fire between two military units

Global Positioning System (GLOH-buhl puh-ZI-shuh-ning SISS-tuhm)—an electronic tool used to find the location of an object; this system is often called GPS

hostage (HOSS-tij)—a person held prisoner by an enemy

obstacle course (OB-stuh-kuhl KORSS)—a series of barriers that a soldier must jump over, climb, or crawl through

retreat (ri-TREET)—to move back or withdraw from a difficult situation

Taliban (TAHL-ee-bahn)—an army in Afghanistan that uses terror in an effort to spread its ideas

terrorist (TER-ur-ist)—someone who uses violence to achieve a goal

READ MORE

David, Jack. *Army Green Berets.* Armed Forces. Minneapolis: Bellwether Media, 2009.

Hamilton, John. *Special Forces.* Defending the Nation. Edina, Minn.: ABDO Pub. Co., 2007.

Nobleman, Marc Tyler. *Green Berets in Action.* Special Ops. New York: Bearport Pub., 2008.

INTERNET SITES

FactHound offers a safe, fun way to find Internet sites related to this book. All of the sites on FactHound have been researched by our staff.

Here's all you do:

Visit *www.facthound.com*

Type in this code: 9781429653794

Check out projects, games and lots more at
www.capstonekids.com

INDEX